SUGAR BOUNDARIES

SUGAR BOUNDARIES

A poetry collection.

Veeva

"My life" something that you've never understood & it is now
that I've understood.

Oh my Golden Diamond

Light heath upon me,
A wrath of blight.
Flowers that bloom so often,
From where they survived.

La Figlia

'That's us in thirty years.'
I've heard this said -
By almost everyone
That belongs to my gender.
While the light shines bright on them
And they feel the world belongs to them.
And so, my mom and I often pray,
For that glory;
For we'd want them to succeed.
While that light is still golden
And their luster is not lost in this world's fury.

A mio Fratello

I was a kid once
When so were you.
Remember when we were living at that house
Our father called home?
And as fortune hit us,
We were thrown.
Not to a mansion
But to a house our mom owned.
And then as we behold the way of life
In separation of patriarchy,
We see what unvarnished liberty holds.
And here as we exhaust juvenility,
Our foundation now
Has wood that creaks.

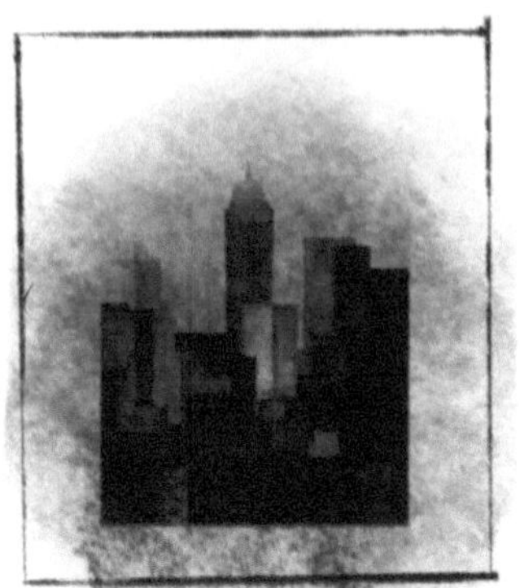

My love

When the rays of sun
Hit your eyes,
They turn brown.
It is a brown I've never seen,
It is a brown your color pallet doesn't have.
I feel it was gods creation
Just for me to steal glances of
And it's love
For every time I see them shine.
It is love
When I see you laugh
For its really just our presence
Keeping us apart.
For all the things you hear wrong,
But I guess them right.
Its love
For all the mischiefs you play
And I am here to be the part of that play.

You & me

That distance of maybe some ten steps
Showed me an unforeseen fate of my life.
As I walk into your arms
As I let myself believe
As I let go of the idea that I lost you.
Since the days bypassed -
A testament to my grief.
As you were fading in dust,
Nigh to something I never reaped.
But now,
As your fingers pass through my hair,
And it's your want to make me breathe air.
It's how we fall to our knees
And let go off the keys
And fall in love with the peace…
Now a state of our lives -
They call, 'A you & me.'

Honey & ice

Get me wasted
But not of alcohol.
It's a want,
Maybe to stop feeling myself.
A want,
To lose myself.
Above - losing myself
And so, I go sublime.
Like your golden eyes
Like sweet honey and ice.

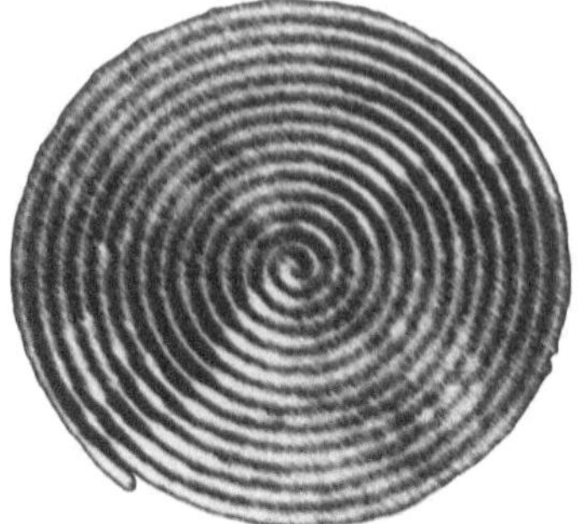

Insanity

I loved it about a minute ago
And now,
The moments gone and I don't see it anymore.
It's gold - as you see it
And it is that what you tell me.
But coal - in my eyes
Oh honey, don't you see my insanity?
I'm 'this' today
Maybe a 'that' tomorrow
But I never see your love fading
While I'm here
Withering in my sorrow.
I'm not so firm today,
Maybe I'll lance some strings that lead to my heart,
And hold your hands
While I end your play
Of which
I'm a part.

Tactics

I know it was nothing
Yet I cried
And it swelled my eyes.
And it's always nothing -
Something my brain surmised.
It is like when pins prick
And there's a fickle smear of angst
For it's so small and yet it draws blood
And you won't cry
Though it ensures a certain presence.
That lament; won't need days to heal
Though it leaves a lesion.

Onus

For it is the weight of my own world
I carry on my shoulders.
These lengths I walk on
 -they are wooden floors.
My shoes on grass
 -Made of leather he stole.
Like big pictures you paint
For which my heart is over its brain.
Are you with me in my future?
Or am I sending flowers for a grave?
My quests
 -even I'm bored of.
The world consumes me.
For I see many golden leaves
And they are falling from their trees.
But the you
 -I cannot lie,
 I see you like a god
 But you are fog.
'Many of these days will come & go'
My brother says that is all.
I am a stone on your land
 -tomorrow of sand, yest made of gold.
But the life in me
 -cant let go.

Ceaseless

In the process of hating you,
I'm here,
Endlessly
In love with you.
My love,
Tell me
In the process of loving you,
Will I start hating you?

Extremes

Into the dark I go
Darker than the ocean's bed.
Into the bright you go
Brighter than the suns own death.

Your Regret

No, but when she drinks, It's tragic.
And her future is lost
In the laments of yesterday.
Her indulgence -
In the name of voices, she can't seem to forget.
And I'm not privy to them
For she never put faces on them
Or doesn't seem to remember them.
So, did I become her regret?
I call her but she hangs up
And she'll call me in a minute again
So, I let that rest.
And in her nights, it's too easy to talk
As we are deceived by the dim light,
It makes you want to tell me
Of all your darks.
I remind her of her vivid past
So, she makes me a part of her art
For yesterday it was new
And today I became all she knew.
Now in my afternoons every day,
I mourn her death
For she's still the same & I couldn't save her doom.
It's September now
And she became
Just one more reason
To hate myself on the day I was born.

Daze

I felt buried under rocks
I thought they would kill me
So, I closed my heart
When our souls met.
And I admit
Your love is a trance.
Your dreamy eyes
Can still make me go blind
It is like a ray of sun,
Wrapped around my heart.
My wind chimes flew in your rain
Hitting on Doors slim on wood
Rotting, like the color grey.
But in my dreams
A hundred and twelve years can fly by,
With my head
Just on your legs
For there's no other way
I'd love to die.

Your coast

What is it that you're holding back?
Or is it just your habits
You try to hide from me?
But I do know who you are,
Maybe someone without an arc.
But you can never lose me
For something that you do
And I choose to hold on to that string
As if it is a vein through which I breathe.
I know
With yourself,
You believe I'm your demon
And in your dreams,
I'm scorching you in dust
You see me, who's taking your life away
And in truth I say
Your coast is the only place
To which my soul makes a way.

My Evermore

The nature to me is bare
No forms, just some colors of despair.
Yet through your eyes
It's like something I've never seen.
Allure - your form,
Pointing me to your blues and greens.
While in silence, I'm standing
To your ignorance complying.
It is your love for which
I fail and I fall.
And I fail miserably
To a fall for only me to weep my tears.
And for every day I sit as a spectator
Lacking words to phrase my failure.
For fast as it comes and faster it goes
A trust broken in a soul.
Yet out of such necessities
I still hold.
And yet you just let it go.

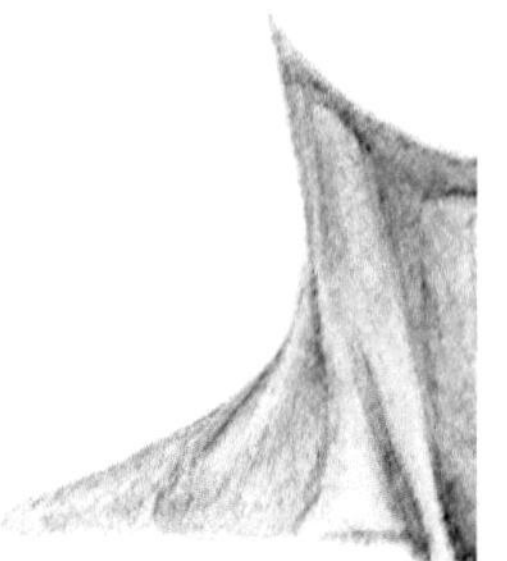

Impuissant

I shut the door quietly
And he cut my heart mildly
And now, he's gone.
And I rage with my eyes loudly
Stripping my soul entirely.

Sour Quests

Am I
The silent soldier
The forgotten lad with a gun?
Who dies for you everyday
With not a portrait of me
And no odes to my glory.
So, in my silence I grieve
And it's always a flat bed with a thick sheet
With a woman by side
And she thinks she makes me complete.
As I close my eyes,
My corse
Dies with the weight
Of some fifty bricks.
And I think of the days I bleed,
Of the wounds
- a gratuity by you
- am I sold?

Saving Grace

It has been times too many that I've saved you
And now I think
It is a dream to get away from you.
And as one's brain fools them,
Your disgrace is now my habitat.
But as I tell you so,
You don't have to bruise me till I get red
For you've already turned my soul black.
And that look in your eyes -
Are they still asking furthermore!
Oh my lord, how come you still don't know?
It's a hope to believe that it is your blindness.
As every day,
Is an ode to your sterling ignorance.
So, I've been led to believe that it's not educated.
Hence saving me from death
As diversely, I refuse to live.
But the land I walk on keeps a mark,
And my years have passed.
So, it's this I've understood -
'My silence'
An answer -
Strong,
To heave the burden of all wrong.

Oh Noble, help me find myself again
Help me see the light again.
My hands are sucked in camaraderie.
And 'I' - the sacrifice
I lost at merger.
Is there a way back to me?
I've lost my faith in the worlds bliss
And I'm now a fool as I pass through this.
What is this truth I seek?
Am I lost in you
Or in negligence - from you?
But I see no 'light'; a way back to me.
Why can't I find this glory?
Oh Noble, help me
Find myself again.

You, now an Exile.

So now, we don't look in the eye
Now it's just a way we speak,
Filled with lies.
Since you asked me, why I speak like this to you.
Why do I feel like I've lost you?
I say where were you
When you cast off your little love noose?
Does it hurt to see me aloof?
My brain which is not yours anymore,
Do you miss me in your midday blues?
Was I asleep? I don't think so.
It's all you did,
Everything,
The way you looked, the way you breathed,
The way you talked,
Just blinding me with glares you released.
Your fingers leaving sparks,
As they reminisced me as a point in the past.
You lifting the scale of voices crossing walls afar,
Crushing a stable foundation
Built on years living life at large.
You lifting a hand,
That burned memories of us in seconds apart.
I was so shrill, I spoke tones,
But my ears just stayed afloat.

Where were you that day?
When you did all this.
Where were you that day
When you said it didn't matter?
What a waste of time!
I; a glass left to shatter.
You can forget me; I will forget you too.
You are nothing to my world
'Just throw yourself off the roof.'
You left me there
With my heart
Just bleeding shades of red despair on gravel stone.
You broke me that day
But my eyes didn't grieve
They didn't shed tears heralding a loss of love that day
Now just a past yet to heave.
My heart didn't stop working that day
It mourned for a life now gone,
Tired of pumping blood to a lifeless form.
My skin didn't get scared that day.
It burned my bones underneath,
Since they left holding on to the ground that day.
I was better lying on dust
Than making my way through mud.
In all ways I feel I stopped worrying that day
For life now, is a path less road anyway.

A duty to fall

Standing here for hours
I see my tears have now fled by
And so has my time.
All those hopes
And all those brawls
Are Nothing.
Yet everything has asked an ownership
As I,
A 'something' they seemed to seek.
So here,
I see me,
Through the world
And its picturesque beauty of it all
And that quintessential duty to fall.

And I lived years

Within that night.

But my memories never lie.

Tell me that I'm right.

My Pygmy Graves

You always open that door
Wishing to find something,
But you never do.
And I always watch you leave
With empty hands & eyes raging in grief
As I, never yield.
And so, these echoes of emptiness
Fill the void of our home
With the walls taller & the doors in myriad.
He is someone who walks outside our house every day,
And tells me of the picture we paint.
It's almost perfect, he says,
As he looks into my eyes
And tells me he sees no pain.
So, I'm in this garden of yours today
And see your hundred plants in the way.
As I walk through the cloaks of your grace
And paths of stones so nicely engraved.
Some hundred yards of acceptance
For the eyes of the human race.
But with each step the light on the trail fades
And with every stone you paved
I see a garden blooming with my Pygmy graves.

It's a search

I'm still searching for an answer.

Should I find a way to live?
But honey again, you'll break me apart
I know the way you love my heart.
I'm so red now, I burn myself to touch.
And the one that loved me,
Is still out on a search.
What will I answer him?
Who is it that broke me?
How will I look him in the eyes?
What will I tell him?
Maybe that I've forgotten how to breathe.
I was a free bird when I met him
And now I've caged myself in
And this edge, is now a drug to me
So then, how will I let you in?
It's that puzzle I look in your eyes
Why do I never solve it?
But my love tells me
You'll see the truth
And asks me to wait for him.
Someday far in eternity
And then you'll live again
Not questioning your mortality.
What if I never see this truth?
Will I die in this cage?
For it's still a search
For when I lose this edge and let you in.

Escape

He said I like the way you talk
And I like the way
You write about your dreams.
I wish could stand a feet down
And hold you in all your glory.
But how'd I lose a man like this?
You remind me of my broken dreams.
Maybe he forgot what he saw in me.
And now you hate the way I talk
And maybe you even hate the way I breathe.
I'd say
I'll meet you again
But I'll never come back-
It's that what I mean.

Sugar Boundaries

These days I am sitting by myself,
There is nothing that this place can find for me.
I am not surprised,
I guess I have given up on life
A place where I find myself to be.
Oh, these doors are wide open
But, where is my heart!
I am looking through these windows
And feeling caged and apart.
Oh love, I need you,
But guess you never saw that
Since you never came through.
Now that breeze has me leaving
I guess that is how I will stop remembering me.
And I know they only mind
When you are not acting in the ways that are so keen.
Why do I sound like a child?
Noticing these peoples wild.
Oh love, I don't need love.
Guess you already knew that
Since you never came through till the very end.
I am standing here with mud on my feet,
That is how you leave me.

We were never there, so it'll never bear.
The bricks
Of guilt,
Let me carry them for you.
Oh love, I don't need you, but I love you.
And I know you know that
Since you never came through
And I'm here, alone.
It's my end.
My mum will be happy
She birthed a child,
I wasn't supposed to live on the day of my demise.
And there's cause in the duty,
As that's his job and it fools me.
Whose morals are at question
When all you do is, bask in the sun.
Oh love, I love you.
But I know you already knew that from a distance.
You capture walls that hide these fears.
How's life, from the bleachers?
Seeing me fail in every sector.
Yet I'll miss you,
But you already knew that.
Since you never came through
And now
I'm here
In the end.

So
I cried
at the end
because I never lost faith.

Undefeated

I feel too alone to continue this fight.
Why am I not even theirs
For even who are mine?
Am I a lonely star?
Or maybe a ship sailed apart?
Oh, It's a high praise,
I'm not even somebody's fading scar.
I'm the stone left on the ground
And my blood dries
But the gods cry to clean it out.
And when the season ends,
I'm bare again
And every man says that's the new fare.
So young and fair.
So, I'm off to the sales again.
Maybe someday,
I'll meet myself again.

Whole

The present, apathetic
Between the truce of our hands now.
Yet our past, a witness
To every smile etched on my face -
A sonnet to your love I sang aloud.
But as a tree sheds its grief,
The winds of autumn
Have taken the rotten fruits our bark heaved.
And maybe I've lost a son
And a daughter for this peace.
Yet I think of the day
When I lay my head on your knees
And our idea of golden horses
As they were galloping through a summer breeze.
I felt, it was all I had
And I'm still there in the nights hard to bear.
And maybe
We are still here,
Running in the winds of spring,
On the rays of sun glazing in.
For I still rejoice with this blessed soul,
For you made me whole.

Paideia

I am
An amalgamation
Of oceans.
I feel I've been raised
By getting drunk on many potions.

She's old now

Now as she stands on her feet
Holding a mass, they can't heed.
With her hair all gray and her eyes all dim.
And when he calls her,
Her eyes wake up
To shine,
Still as the day she first met him.
Though all the glory now gone -
A stance of the verity shown by him.
Yet her life exists while her heart beats
And maybe it's a proof she refuses to accept
For she still has a roof on her head
And her children still breathe.
So, every day in her solace
She asks someone above
Are my mistakes
My only form of shield?

Paradise

My soul has leapt to jump
Off of every cliff you slide.
And as you leap,
I see
Your feathers
Have taken the form of the beautiful sky.
And as my eyes deceive me
They say – it is you
Who never lets me die.
But now I'm already in the middle of the sky
And on the edge of my demise,
I found you there
And felt paradise.

You

The first feelings,
They never came back.
But the Gods know
I kept falling in love with you again and again.

Dedicated to my mother.
I love you.

And to someone with a brush as his art.
Thank you.

Credits:

Edited by - Sanjana Trivedi
Layout by - Sanjana Trivedi

Contact the author at
Email: veeva14005@gmail.com